ck and this is my story. I never

rave person, certainly not a hero. But

there is a hero waiting to emerge.

ithout the h   roes. This

Luba Tryszynska

Luba

The Angel of Bergen-Belsen

Luba
The Angel of Bergen-Belsen

As told to Michelle R. McCann
by Luba Tryszynska-Frederick
Illustrations by Ann Marshall

TRICYCLE PRESS

Berkeley | Toronto

For Ronan, my angel. And for Jerry, my love. —MRM

For Jerry Stern and Ruth Saltzman with gratitude, and for All and Patty with love. —LT-F

To Mom and Dad. —AM

Author's Note

Luba: The Angel of Bergen-Belsen is a biographical story based on actual events that occurred during Luba Tryszynska-Frederick's life. The named individuals, dates, places, and poems used in the text are real. Dialogue and a few composite characters have been created in order to better tell the story. During the Holocaust, many different groups of orphaned children were protected by caring prisoners in concentration camps, including Bergen-Belsen. The children in this story were Dutch; their fathers were diamond cutters from Amsterdam who were relocated to Bergen-Belsen to help the Nazi war effort. These sons and daughters came to be known as "the Diamond Children":

Greta Aandagt	Flora le Grand	Jacob Polak
Ronald Abram	Ellie Groen	Sarah Polak
Nanette Blitz	Esther Groen	Gerrit van Praag
Robert Blitz	Klara Hagedus	Schoontje Prins
Donald Lopes Cardozo	Ellie Hamburger	Helena Rabbie
Judy Lopes Cardozo	Lion Kleerekoper	Maurice Rabbie
Mirjam Lopes Cardozo	Marcus Kleerekoper	Phietje Rabbie
Maurice Cohen	Gerard Lakmaker	Isabella D. Rijxman
Samuel Cohen	Connie Lehmann	Isaac Cohen Rodrigues (Jack)
Gerrit Cohensius	Erica Lehmann	Rachel Cohen Rodrigues
Sylvia Coster	Oscar Lehmann	Magareta Slap
Estella M. Degen	Toni Lehmann	Robert H. Slap
Marcus Degen	Henneke Maandag	Alicia T. Vos
Simon Degen	Simon Maandag	Paula Vos
Levie van Embden	Sammy Monteira	Ronald Weening
Andree Engelander	Emanuel Neeter	Hetty Werkendam
Philip de Goede	Helena A. Pinkhof	Jackie Werkendam
Fina le Grand	Hendrika Polak	Max Werkendam

*My mother always told me that she gave birth to me,
but that Luba gave me life.*

—Stella Degen-Fertig (Estella Degen), the youngest child rescued by Luba

Prologue

In the 1930s, a political group called the "National Socialist German Workers' Party" rose to power in Germany. Soon to be known as the Nazi Party, they built giant prisons called "concentration camps," where, at first, they locked up common criminals and people who disagreed with their politics. Next, the Nazis declared that anyone who was different from their ideal, who was not a Nazi or what they called "Aryan" (blonde-haired, blue-eyed Caucasians of northern European descent), was an enemy of Germany. They arrested Gypsies, people with physical and mental disabilities, Jehovah's Witnesses, homosexuals, and Jewish people and put them in the camps as well.

In 1938, Nazi troops began invading other European countries: Austria, Czechoslovakia, Poland, Denmark, Norway, Belgium, Holland, Luxembourg, France, Yugoslavia, Greece, and the Soviet Union. World War II was underway, and as the Nazi troops spread, their concentration camps filled with Jews and other non-Aryans from all over Europe.

For years, the rest of the world believed what the Nazis told them: The prisoners were in "work camps" building things the Germans needed to win the war. But something more evil was going on. The Nazis were secretly killing their prisoners.

Our story is set in one of these concentration camps. Located between two German villages, it was called Bergen-Belsen. This is the true story of one Jewish heroine—Luba Tryszynska, "the Angel of Bergen-Belsen."

Luba lay in her bunk with her eyes closed. Outside, the night was cold and moonless, yet inside, the drafty prison barracks weren't much warmer. It was Luba's first night in this strange, new camp. She had no home, no family, and questions plagued her sleep: *Why am I still alive? Why was I spared?*

Half dreaming, she thought she heard her son Isaac calling her, "Mama! Mama!" But she knew Isaac wasn't there.

Luba sat up. "Do you hear that?" she whispered to Hermina, who shared her bunk. "Children crying."

"Only your first night and already you are hearing things?" Hermina rolled her eyes. "You are just dreaming. Go to sleep. The Nazis don't like crazy people, you know."

Luba tried to sleep, but the voices returned, "Mama! Mama!"

Who is crying? she wondered. Luba wrapped a thin blanket around her shoulders and went out into the frozen night.

Outside, she could barely see the snow-covered ground, but the cries were clearer. They led her behind the barracks, to an empty field. That's where she found them: fifty-four children huddled together like lost ducklings.

Some were just babies tucked into pillowcases.

"Where are your parents?" Luba asked the biggest child, whose name was Jack.

"G . . . gone," he stammered. "They took them away."

"How did you get here?"

"A truck. I heard the drivers talking . . . they were supposed to take us to the woods and. . . ." Jack stopped and stared at his feet.

"And what?" Luba coaxed.

"And shoot us," he whispered.

Luba reached out and stroked his hair until he continued.

"They had an argument. One driver wouldn't do it, so they left us here instead. He said the cold would kill us anyway." Jack peeked up at Luba. "We haven't eaten all day."

The rest of the children stared at Luba and she heard the question in her mind again: *Why was I spared?* This time she thought she knew the answer.

She gathered the group together and led them back to the barracks, following her trail of muddy footprints through the snow.

"You really are crazy!" Hermina cried. Now everyone was awake.

"Where will we put them?"

"How will we feed them?"

Luba answered their questions with one of her own: "What if they were your children?"

Another woman agreed, "Wouldn't you want someone to help them?"

"Of course," the others replied. "But if the guards find out we are keeping them, they will kill us!"

The women stared at the children for a long, long time. Finally, an older prisoner broke the silence, "Come, little ones. Find a bed."

Perhaps the others remembered that it was the season of Hanukkah and thought of their own lost families, for they too called softly, "Yes, welcome. Welcome."

The already crowded room was quickly overwhelmed with children lying three to a bunk. As the women busied themselves tucking in their new guests, Luba sang a lullaby. One by one, the children closed their eyes, until every child was asleep. All except the oldest girl, Hetty.

"Do you have any children?" Hetty asked Luba.

"I have a young son," she answered. "His name is Isaac."

"Where is he?"

Luba hesitated. "I'm not sure."

"What happened to him?"

"So many questions for such a young girl," Luba sighed, but she kept talking.

"Before the war I lived in Poland, near the Russian border, on a farm with my parents and my brothers and sisters." Luba could see the patchwork fields in her mind—the cabbage and beets and carrots, the small vegetable garden outside the kitchen. She rubbed her eyes.

"When I married, my husband Herschel and I moved to a nearby town. There Isaac was born. We didn't have many things, but we were all so happy together.

"Then one day the Nazi soldiers came. They took us away to the camp at Auschwitz."

She didn't want to tell Hetty about the train ride. How everyone whispered that it was a death camp they were headed to. She didn't want to tell Hetty that the moment the train pulled into Auschwitz, Herschel was taken to the men's camp and guards tore Isaac from her arms. She didn't want to tell Hetty that she could still hear him calling "Mama! Mama!" even though two years had passed.

Instead she told Hetty, "I am lucky. The Nazis believe I am a nurse and sent me here to help take care of their wounded soldiers." But the girl's eyes were finally closed. "And now I have found someone else's children."

The next morning, fifty-four stomachs were rumbling, but Luba was gone. "Where is she?" the children whispered to each other.

Suddenly, the door flew open. "Quickly, take this," Luba called to Hermina, handing her a steaming pot. Seconds later she returned with another.

As the hungry children gathered around, Luba pulled off the hot lids with her skirt.

"Porridge!" they marveled.

For months the children had lived on nothing but cold, watery soup made with bits of moldy carrots and parsnips.

The women shook their heads as they watched the children devour every last spoonful. How did Luba do it? Extra food was nearly impossible to find, even for one person. But enough for more than fifty hungry mouths? Surely, it was a miracle.

It was a miracle Luba performed for months during that winter. To get food for the children, Luba had to walk across the camp to the kitchen area twice a day, and each time she had to pass through a gate guarded by Nazi soldiers.

Of all the prisoners in the concentration camps, Jews were treated the worst. Most were forbidden to go anywhere without permission. But camp nurses, like Luba, had some freedom to move around. Luckily, the sleeves of Luba's uniform hid the numbers tattooed there by the Nazis, identifying her as a Jew. And since the guards assumed this pretty nurse, who spoke fluent German and Russian, was merely a political prisoner, she wasn't going to correct their mistake.

Still, Luba was terrified during that walk. She prayed they wouldn't check her arm and send her back to the barracks empty-handed—or worse.

"Guten Tag," Luba greeted the guards, smiling as she waited for them to let her pass.

"Ja, ja," they answered, motioning her through the gate. Sometimes they smiled back.

"Danke," called Luba, giving them a cheerful wave to disguise her shaking hands.

Once inside the kitchen area, Luba would first visit the bakery. The prisoners were given only leftovers—stale, half-eaten loaves. But one woman who helped make the bread was a Jewish prisoner.

"Don't you have some bread for my children today?" Luba asked the woman. Many prisoners at Bergen-Belsen knew about Luba's children and could be trusted not to tell the Nazi guards her secret. But sneaking the children food was a more dangerous matter.

The woman shook her head and grumbled, "Why do you care about these children? They are not yours."

"But they are someone's children," Luba reminded her, "and they are hungry."

She smiled as the woman tucked two warm loaves into her coat.

In another building she would visit the butcher, a Russian political prisoner who prepared meat for the guards. Luba felt nervous asking for his help because he was not Jewish, but the children hadn't eaten meat in months.

"Impossible!" snapped the old man, shaking his head. "I cannot give you sausage. The guards would kill me if I got caught—and you, too!"

"But comrade," Luba pleaded in Russian, "I give you my word—if they catch me, I will tell them I stole it."

The butcher thought for a moment, then shook his head again. "No, it is too much risk."

"Ah well, I thought you were a grandfather," Luba sighed, turning to leave, "but I must have been mistaken. A grandfather would never let someone else's grandchildren go hungry."

The butcher stormed past her and through the door, puffing with anger.

But when Luba left, she noticed a large stick of salami tucked behind a box. The butcher was a grandfather after all.

Luba pushed the sausage inside her bulging coat.

Last, she would go to the cook who was in charge of all the food for Bergen-Belsen. He was the hardest one for Luba to face. He was German, locked up for some earlier crime, and he didn't like the Jewish prisoners any more than the guards did. If he reported her to his Nazi supervisor, she would be killed.

"Don't you have just a bit of potato soup for some little ones in my barracks?" she begged him.

"Ha! There isn't extra soup for anyone!" said the cook, laughing harshly. "Why should I give any to your dirty Jewish children?"

Luba was so furious she turned to leave, but the cook called to her, "You are a brave one. You remind me of my wife."

Luba snapped back, "Surely your wife would be better at getting the soup, no?"

The cook laughed again and pinched Luba's cheek. "You sound even braver when you are angry. Oh, give them the dregs—what do I care?" He poured the last of the soup into her pot.

Luba had wanted to slap his hand away from her face, but instead she smiled and hid the pot inside her magical coat.

From abandoned buildings around camp, Luba collected scraps of wood. When it got very cold, she would light a fire in the stove to warm the children, but only after dark when no one could see the smoke.

Sometimes Luba convinced the guards' wives to give her extra clothes and blankets. She didn't tell them why, and if they knew about Luba's children, they didn't say a word.

Whenever the children got sick, Luba went to a Jewish doctor for help. There wasn't much besides aspirin and bandages, but it was enough.

Whatever the children needed, Luba found it. Every day she risked her life to keep them alive. She just hoped someone might be doing the same for Isaac somewhere.

The other women in the barracks did their part to care for the children as well. They cooked the food Luba brought and helped the youngest ones get dressed. They used one wet cloth to keep fifty-four children as clean as they could.

The children also helped. They did chores, told each other stories, acted out plays, and traveled to make-believe lands. But they never, ever cried. None of them could forget being left in that cold, dark field.

At the end of each day, the children gathered around the door waiting for Luba, praying she hadn't been caught.

And each time she walked through the door, exhausted from her search, they would whisper, "Sister Luba! You're back! You're back!" As they rubbed her tired feet, Luba's strength would return, and she would remember again why she had been spared.

As the days grew warmer and spring approached, the children began planning a birthday surprise for Luba.

There were certain prisoners at Bergen-Belsen who could make trades for special items—jewelry for bread, cigarettes for medicine. Luckily, there was a Dutch prisoner who had just what they wanted, but it wouldn't be cheap—two entire loaves of bread.

"Where will we get the bread?" sighed Jack.

"I have an idea," whispered Hetty. "But everyone will have to pitch in."

Hetty knew that a loaf of bread had seventeen slices in it. And every day, Luba gave each child in the barracks one slice of bread. If Hetty and Jack could convince the children to give up half a slice of their daily bread, they could buy Luba's present in just two nights.

The rest of the children thought it was a brilliant plan, and soon they had a pile of bread. Although their stomachs growled, the children were so excited they hardly noticed.

"Surprise!" cried the children when Luba opened the door.

"What is all this?" she asked, amazed at the scrubbed and rosy faces grinning before her.

"It's your birthday!" said Jack.

Luba hadn't even remembered. She had spent hours looking for food with no luck and feared tonight would be a hungry night for everyone.

All of the children lined up in front of Luba, each with a small gift for her—little things they had made themselves from scraps of paper and cloth, bits of string and wood. The last girl in line handed Luba a heart-shaped box, wrapped in cloth cut from the bottom of Hetty's dress. Luba lifted the lid.

Inside she found a red silk scarf. "It's beautiful," Luba exclaimed, but it wasn't the final gift.

As Hetty unfolded a piece of paper, the room turned quiet. "This is a birthday poem we wrote for you:

Sister Luba, the name fits like a glove.
You have all our respect and all of our love.
From early morning till late at night,
Not once do you let us out of your sight.
The day has barely begun,
And already Sister Luba is on the run.
Our lives are in her hands, we know full well,
And all of us are grateful, big and small.
We wish you joy, health, and happiness,
And may freedom come quickly for all of us."

There were no voices in Luba's head now. No questions. For the first time since they took Isaac away, she was happy to be alive.

Her happiness didn't last long, however. Rumors were flying: The Nazis were losing the war. The news brought joy to the prisoners, but not to the guards, who began treating them even worse than before. There was very little food. There was no medicine.

Every day the children got more and more hungry, until they couldn't even feel their hunger anymore. And soon many of them were sick.

One evening Luba looked around the barracks. The children were so thin. Many were suffering from typhus, a disease that had already killed thousands of prisoners. Their high fevers made them so tired they couldn't sit up. Even the children who weren't sick lay in their bunks, too weak to play. At this rate, they wouldn't last another week.

"What am I going to do?" Luba worried.

"Sister Luba, please don't cry." It was Jack. "Don't worry," he said, wrapping a skinny arm around Luba's shoulders. "We will make it."

"I know we will, Jack. I know we will." But Luba wasn't so sure.

The next morning Luba awoke to a strange rumbling. *Thunder? Another airplane attack?* She pushed open the barracks door. Camp was deserted. The guards were gone, and at the camp entrance huge tanks rolled through the gates.

Am I dreaming? Luba wondered.

Just then, loudspeakers atop each tank barked out, "You are free! You are free!" The British army had arrived. The war was over.

"Children, wake up!" cried Luba.

When the British soldiers looked in Luba's door, they couldn't believe their eyes. Inside the dark barracks, they saw a few women prisoners surrounded by swarms of children. There were children in the bunks, children under the table, children tugging at their uniforms.

The children looked up at the soldiers with dark, sunken eyes and smiles that could light up the entire camp.

The soldiers were baffled. "How did all these children survive the war?"

Surely, it was a miracle.

Now Luba had no need for her magical coat. As she took it off, the sun warmed the arms she no longer had to hide. Luba and the other women scooped up the weakest children, while the stronger ones held onto their skirts.

"We are free," Luba said as they made their way past the barbed wire and through the unguarded gate. "We are free."

Epilogue

During those last months in Bergen-Belsen more than half the sixty thousand prisoners died of starvation and illness. Yet of the original fifty-four Dutch children that Luba rescued on that cold December night in 1944, fifty-two survived through the end of the war in April 1945.

After the liberation, the children refused to be separated from Luba, so she escorted them to Holland. By the time they arrived, Luba was a national hero. The Dutch people called her "the Angel of Bergen-Belsen." The children were reunited with their surviving family members and Queen Wilhelmina herself asked Luba to stay in Holland, promising she would be taken care of for the rest of her life. But Luba didn't stay. Once the Dutch children were safe, she returned to Bergen-Belsen. She wanted to help care for other orphaned children who had been transferred there at the end of the war and she also wanted to find her own relatives. All over Europe, survivors of the war were living in refugee camps, having lost their homes, their jobs, and all their money. While Luba was certain that Herschel and Isaac were dead, she held out hope that in one of these refugee camps she might find other members of her family.

When the remaining orphans in Bergen-Belsen were relocated to other countries, she escorted one group to a refugee camp in Sweden. After much

Luba (top row, second from left) with some of the Diamond Children on the day of Bergen-Belsen's liberation.

searching, however, Luba could find no other living relatives, so in 1947 she emigrated to the United States. There, she married another Holocaust survivor, Sol Frederick, and they had two children together, All and Patty. Yet Luba still thought about the Dutch children every day. *How were they doing? Did they remember her?* For years she heard nothing.

But the children had not forgotten Luba. As soon as they were old enough, they began searching the world for her. Jack was the first to find her, and over the years a few others located her as well. As the fiftieth anniversary of the end of the war approached, they arranged another surprise for Luba.

In April 1995, they flew her to Amsterdam for a reunion. Luba was nearly seventy-five, and the "children" were in their fifties and sixties. But as soon as she stepped off the plane, the years fell away. She was their Luba, and they were her children.

Once again, they had a very special present planned for her. They took her to city hall. Surrounded by television cameras, reporters, the mayor of Amsterdam,

and the children, Queen Beatrix presented Luba with the Silver Medal of Honor for Humanitarian Services for her heroic deeds in Bergen-Belsen. Luba liked it almost as much as her red scarf!

And there was one more surprise. Thanks to all the television coverage, a family in the United States heard about Luba. Her name

Luba (front, center) with some of the surviving Diamond Children at the 1995 fifty-year reunion in Amsterdam.

sounded familiar, so they took a chance. After talking on the phone with her for hours, they discovered they were related through Luba's grandfather. After many long years, Luba had found some of the family she lost during the war.

World War II and the Holocaust

World War II raged across Europe and the Pacific Ocean from 1939 to 1945, but the persecution of the Jewish people began years earlier. In 1933, Adolf Hitler and his followers took power in Germany and used the Jewish people as a scapegoat for the country's problems. He told the German people that they could succeed only if the Jews were destroyed. Many believed him. They quickly made life for their Jewish neighbors nearly impossible: They destroyed Jewish homes and businesses, stole Jewish possessions, and eventually arrested the Jews and sent them to concentration camps. When the German army invaded other European countries, the Jewish citizens of those countries received the same treatment.

By the end of the war, the Nazis had killed six million Jewish men, women, and children in what came to be called "the Holocaust."

More than thiry-five thousand Jewish prisoners died inside Bergen-Belsen alone, including the famous teenage author Anne Frank (she died of typhus, just weeks before the camp's liberation). In fact, conditions were so horrible at Bergen-Belsen that an additional thirteen thousand prisoners died from disease *after* they were set free. The entire camp had to be burned because it was so infested with typhus.

Like Luba, many Jewish survivors of the Holocaust fled Europe after the war. They settled all around the world, in the United States, South America, Canada, and the just-founded Jewish state of Israel. In their new homes, these survivors rebuilt their lives from nothing. Their courage is a light for humanity even now, showing that strength, dignity, and hope can take root in even the darkest of places.

Europe at the start of World War II, including Luba's hometown, Zastovia.

Bibliography

BOOKS:

Bergen-Belsen: Explanatory Notes on the Exhibition. Hanover, Germany: Niedersachsen, 1991.

Gilbert, Martin. *The Holocaust: A History of the Jews of Europe during the Second World War.* New York: Henry Holt, 1986.

Lévy-Hass, Hanna. *Inside Belsen.* Sussex, England: Harvester Press Ltd., 1982.

Lukas, Richard C. *The Forgotten Holocaust: The Poles under German Occupation 1939-1944.* New York: Hippocrene Books, 1997.

Ritvo, Roger A., et al. *Sisters of Sorrow: Voices of Care in the Holocaust.* College Station: Texas A&M University Press, 2000.

Smith, David Michael and Susan Goschie. *The Eyes of an Angel: The Story of the Angel of Bergen-Belsen.* Portland, OR: Personal Saga, 2002.

Verolme, Hetty E. *The Children's House of Belsen.* Fremantle, Australia: Fremantle Arts Centre Press, 2000.

ARTICLES:

Altshuler, Melvin. "'Angel' Who Saved 94—Has Son of Own—A U.S. Citizen." *Washington Post,* 1950.

"'Angel of Belsen' Arrives." *New York Times,* 15 Jan. 1947.

Barnett, Erin H. "'Angel of Bergen-Belsen' Graces Portland with Visit." *Oregonian,* 18 Oct. 2000.

"Belsen Angel Here Seeking Job As a Nurse." *New York Herald Tribune,* 15 Jan. 1947.

Elliott, Lawrence. "A Heroine in Hell." *Reader's Digest,* Nov. 1997: 75-80.

Noyes, Newbold. "Spectres of War Haunt the 'Angel of Belsen.'" *Washington D.C. Sunday Star,* 2 Feb. 1947.

"One of 94 Rescued in '45 Visits 'Angel of Belsen.'" *Washington D.C. Star,* 1957.

Smith, Marie. "'Angel' to Unveil It—Ghetto Uprising Memorial Given." *Washington Post,* 1963.

Tau, Tove. "The Angel of Bergen-Belsen: Rendezvous in Washington with Luba Trychinska." *Aftenposten* [Oslo, Norway], 13 Nov. 1956.

VIDEOS:

"Angel of Belsen" *Dateline.* Narr. Jane Pauley. Sen. Prod. Susan Farkas. NBC. 19 Oct. 1994.

Investigative Reports. Narr. Bill Kurtis. Prod. Loxley-Hall. A&E Television Networks. 14 Mar. 1998.

British soldier inspecting ruined barracks at Bergen-Belsen after liberation.

LETTERS:

Cardozo, Mirjam Lopes. Letter to Luba Tryszynska-Frederick. 18 Apr. 1994.

Collis, F. Letter of Commendation for Luba Tryszynska-Frederick from the War Organisation of the British Red Cross Society. 30 July 1945.

Lehmann, Erica. Letter to Luba Tryszynska-Frederick. 1995.

Pinkhof, Helena. Letter to Luba Tryszynska-Frederick. 1 Jan. 1997.

Werkendam, Jackie. Letter to Luba Tryszynska-Frederick. 10 Nov. 1946.

PERSONAL INTERVIEWS:

Lakmaker, Gerard. Email interviews. Fall 2002 and spring 2003.

Rodrigues, Jack. Telephone interviews. Spring 2003.

Tryszynska-Frederick, Luba. Personal interview. 6 and 8 Oct. 2000.

WEBSITES:

United States Holocaust Memorial Museum—www.ushmm.org

Simon Wiesenthal Center and Museum of Tolerance www.wiesenthal.com

Museum of Jewish Heritage: A Living Memorial to the Holocaust www.mjhnyc.org

Los Angeles Museum of the Holocaust—www.jewishla.org

Yad Vashem Holocaust Martyrs' and Heroes' Remembrance Memorial (Israel)—www.yad-vashem.org.il

Imperial War Museum's Holocaust Exhibit (England) www.iwm.org.uk/lambeth/holoc-ex1.htm

Acknowledgments

I would like to thank the following people for helping bring Luba's story to life: Ruth Saltzman, for introducing me to Luba and for your enormous assistance every step of the way; Jerry Stern, for your help with translations and crucial fact-checking; Jack Rodrigues and Gerard Lakmaker for your additional fact-checking assistance; Emunah Herzog, for being such a wonderful support for Luba and a liaison for me; Laura Carlsmith, my writing partner, for reading this story a thousand times, making it so much better, and always keeping my spirits up; Ellen Howard, for your inspiration and invaluable writing expertise; Jamie and Charlotte, my sisters, for your always honest input; Ivo Trummer, my brother-in-law, for his knowledge of and help with WWII and Holocaust history; my editor, Summer Dawn Laurie, for making the words something I'm proud of; and Nicole Geiger, my publisher, for your belief in the book and your passion to get Luba's story out to the world. Thank you all!

The publisher is grateful to Adaire J. Klein, Director of Library and Archival Services at the Simon Wiesenthal Center and Museum of Tolerance, for her expert and careful review of this book.

Text copyright © 2003 by Michelle R. McCann
Illustrations copyright © 2003 by Ann Marshall

Tricycle Press
a little division of Ten Speed Press
P.O. Box 7123
Berkeley, California 94707
www.tenspeed.com

Design by Nancy Austin
Typeset in Cloister Oldstyle
The illustrations in this book were rendered in oil and collage.

Picture Credits
Epilogue (left): courtesy of AP/Wide World Photos
Epilogue (medal): Cantoo, Inc.
World War II map: copyright © 1999 maps.com
Bibliography: National Archives, Suitland MD, courtesy of the United States Holocaust Memorial Museum
Back cover: Rick Rappaport Photography

Library of Congress Cataloging-in-Publication Data

McCann, Michelle Roehm, 1968-
  Luba : the angel of Bergen-Belsen / as told to Michelle R. McCann by Luba Tryszynska-Frederick ; illustrated by Ann Marshall.
    p. cm.
Summary: A biography of the Jewish heroine, Luba Tryszynska, who saved the lives of more than fifty Jewish children in the Bergen-Belsen concentration camp during the winter of 1944/45.
  ISBN 1-58246-098-1
  1. Tryszynska-Frederick, Luba. 2. Jewish women in the Holocaust--Biography--Juvenile literature.
3. Jewish children in the Holocaust--Netherlands--Juvenile literature. 4. Holocaust, Jewish (1939-1945)--Netherlands--Juvenile literature. [1. Tryszynska-Frederick, Luba. 2. Heroes. 3. Holocaust, Jewish (1939-1945). 4. Jews--United States--Biography. 5. Women--Biography.]
I. Marshall, Ann E., ill. II. Title.
D804.34 .M34 2003
940.53'18'092--dc21

            2003000543

First Tricycle Press printing, 2003
Printed in Singapore

1 2 3 4 5 6 — 07 06 05 04 03